The Still Voice Inside

A Faith-Based Meditation Journey

by Joe Bamisile

CREATIVE MINDS PUBLICATIONS

Testimonials

Joe has a gift to help people create space in this busy world for what matters most. I've watched him train men to practice intentional pauses that prioritize the important over the urgent. I'd highly recommend this resource to anyone feeling the busyness of life.

Brandon Samuel
Senior Pastor
The Chapel

As a journalist, I had the fortunate opportunity to interview Joe while working on a mental health series called "You Are Not Alone." His story was not only inspiring, but relatable to so many young people struggling to find acceptance in a post-Covid, social media driven world. I was so impressed with Joe's faith based approach to mental wellness, that I asked if he could speak to my daughter's senior class at their convocation ceremony. His speech was so unscripted, quick-witted and sincere that the graduates hung on his every word. Simply put, Joe has a remarkable ability to help people feel less alone in their struggles, while giving them the tools to overcome.

Tracy Sears
Anchor/ Reporter
CBS 6

Joe is able to write, speak, and share his personal testimony with such authenticity and vulnerability. He is wise beyond his years and inspires others as a powerful role model. He is open and transparent about his highs and lows and his setbacks and challenges in such a way that he deeply connects with his audience and immediately builds trust through his story. Joe's testimony is one of perseverance and resilience, and his testimony is truly an inspiration to others.

Emily Weinstein
VP of Development
First Tee - Greater Richmond

Joe is a young leader who is spiritually mature beyond his years. He places the highest priority in his everyday life to quieting himself before God, so he can sense how God is guiding his next steps. His ability to be a leader of leaders is engaging and thought provoking!

Randy Webb
Director of Kingdom Builders
The Chapel

To My Mother,
Your prayers have done more than you could
ever imagine.

Table of Contents

Preface

In today's fast-paced world, sitting still and doing "nothing" is often seen as wasteful. In many Western societies, especially in the United States, taking a rest from the business of life is a tough swim against the racing current of cultural norms. Despite this disposition, over the past two and a half years, I've spent one thousand hours doing exactly what many would perhaps consider "nothing"... meditating.

From January 17, 2023, to June 1, 2025 (a total of 866 consecutive days), I spent one to two daily meditating.

At seven years old, I was first introduced to meditation by my grandfather. He had found that meditation brought him peace, joy, and a deeper sense of fulfillment beyond life's circular routines. But meditation wasn't *just* about escaping stress. It helped him to build a more meaningful connection to the world beyond what he could see around him.

The first time I joined Him; something shifted within me. As we sat together in stillness, I felt connected to a spiritual realm. In these moments of silence and intentionality, I found a unique beauty in simply *being*. In detaching from the distractions, noise, and the constant pull of the outside world, I felt grounded. Taken aback and intrigued by the experience, I began meditating almost every day.

However, as I grew older, I became disengaged. At the age of sixteen, I subconsciously began chasing everything the world deemed valuable or worthy. As time passed, I found myself subtly starting to believe that spirituality and faith, of any kind, was just an antique of the past. As I chased success, status, approval, and pressure to always be the best, I ignored the parts of my soul that yearned, and were designed, for spiritual connection. In hindsight, I believe that the neglect of my spiritual life opened the door to anxiety, insecurity, and an unending need to fit in. Instead of accepting an invitation to true peace, I had invited so many counterfeit Gods into my life, resulting in constant emotional and mental pain.

Fooled by the lies of society, I attempted to drown out everything with drugs and unhealthy relationships. The more I chased what the world said would fulfill me, the emptier I felt and turned to vices.

My relationships were shallow, the joy was temporary, and eventually, I lost complete sight of what mattered. Having no sense of God in my life led me to the belief that everything was meaningless. My purpose to live was diminished. I felt lonely, constantly stressed, yet unfilled all at the same time. What started as excitement turned into depression, anxiety, and isolation.

I kept telling myself I was in control, but deep down, I knew I was not. Therapy helped me to identify and name the pain, but ultimately, I craved true answers and solutions.

Things finally shifted after my dad nearly died and I could see my mother, for the first time in my life, visibly struggling. The weight of seeing my parents in distress exposed how fragile my life had become. The therapy and coping tools I leaned on were not strong enough to hold me.

By the grace of God, soon after all of this happened, I was unintentionally led to read the Bible by a stranger. I started reading daily which led me to having a relationship with Jesus Christ in a way I did not know was possible. In a few short months, I released the need to be liked, I stopped the drugs, walked away from relationships that were unhealthy, and began healing through Him. For the first time, I was not chasing: I was living authentically.

My newfound belief and submission to Jesus led to me placing Jesus in the center of my meditations. After a year or so of this reordering, I had inexplicable peace in my mind, genuine friendships, freedom from all the things that were causing pain. While all these changes were blessings, the ultimate prize was my relationship with Jesus Christ.

I realized that sharing what I had learned with others was far more valuable than keeping it as a personal experience. Fellowship with the Lord in silence has completely shaped how I approach life, and it has also increased how much I trust the Lord. Sitting in silence with the Lord is still something I do daily, and one I hope to share with others who are seeking peace, purpose, and a deeper relationship to their faith.

***

For better or for worse, meditation carries a stigma. It's often associated with a particular religion like Buddhism or Hinduism while other times, it is dismissed as something for hippies, the overly spiritual, or people seeking a trendy mental health fix.

Yet, between 2023 and 2025, I was a college basketball player earning my master's degree, running a business, maintaining a relationship, raising a dog, traveling, conducting scientific research, binge-watching TV, going to the theater a few times a month, and writing this book. I also spent a thousand hours sitting still and doing absolutely "nothing."

I am no saint, guru, or monk. I am an ambitious, hard-working American in my early twenties. I am imperfect. I can be moody. I've made mistakes, have struggles I can't fix, and a future I can't predict. I am not enlightened, nor do I have all the answers. However, I do have something to share—and it's not because I've cracked the code of life or have reached a perfect state of peace. Far from it!

I'm just like you: navigating the chaos of life, chasing dreams, carrying responsibilities, and wrestling with doubts and fears. But through all of this, meditation has been a helpful tool to stay grounded. Setting time aside for meditation created a space to breathe when life felt too heavy, room for clarity when my mind was racing, and peace from the Lord. I believe meditation can do the same for you. Not in some mystical, far-off way, but in a real, tangible sense. It's not about escaping your life, it's about showing up more fully for it.

It's about finding moments of stillness in the noise, slowness in the speed of life, and rest when there seemingly shouldn't be. Meditation creates space between your thoughts while reconnecting you with who you are beyond the roles, goals, and endless to-do lists.

When you meditate, something shifts.

At first, it might just feel like an inexplicable pause or a rare moment where you find yourself not chasing the next thing. Over time, this stillness starts to seep into the rest of your life. You might notice you're less reactive, more patient, and somehow more present, even in the middle of your worst fears. You begin to hear your own thoughts more clearly. By the grace of God, you may even experience a deeper connection to the Lord-a still, small voice beneath the noise.

I'm not promising instant peace or some magical transformation. I am saying that if you give this a chance, make time for nothingness and really lean into the stillness, you might discover something powerful. This isn't just about meditation; it's about finding your way back to yourself, to true peace, and the Lord.

I hope that by the time you reach the end of this book, you also feel a deeper sense of peace within yourself, a calm that isn't shaken by the world around you, and the resilience to move forward knowing there is a place you may always return to. Maybe, just maybe, by the last page, you will be inspired to do "nothing."

My goal in writing this book is to share my experiences, thoughts, images, and insights that I would not have had without meditation. If all I do is plant a seed in your life, that is enough for me.

I want to extend an invitation to everyone to journey alongside me. For some, this book may feel like a testimony. For others, it may offer a small window into the wonders of meditation and mindfulness. There will be moments of confusion, thought-provoking pages, and, at times, unclear answers. I encourage readers to be willing to pause, sit with, reflect on, and accept what each page has to offer. My hope is that these pages will serve as a guide, facilitate growth, and challenge comfortable perspectives. This book is meant to be an experience, whatever form that may take for you.

Using This Book Well

Ironically, given that I'm authoring a book now, I am a learner who doesn't solely retain information by reading a traditional front to back novel. Therefore, the structure, which may at times seem full of randomness, is an authentic format for me to share stories, prayers, poems, biblical resources, and my own thoughts. With this in mind, the seven parts of this book and each page are fully complete by themselves. However, every page is intentionally selected to be a part of the collection. Yet the unity of all 7 parts makes a complete whole together. The book was crafted this way so you may spend as long as you need on any page or on any part. When you finish the book in its entirety, you may always return to what you need. This book is good once. Better twice. Best experienced when it is revisited with regularity.

One notable thing, anything titled "Meditation", is a prayer I wrote over the course of anywhere between 1-100 hours of meditating. I would only write lines down after meditation.

Meditation in the morning allows you to start your day with rest, stillness, peace, quietness, healthy solitude, joy, self-reflection, mindfulness, and slowness. Beginning your day like this sets the tone for everything you will go through, every interaction you will have, and the way in which you will live that day. By doing seemingly nothing, you are putting your day in God's hands. His doing is better seen when we do nothing. Praying before meditation helps you to quiet your mind. Praying directly after meditating gives you the opportunity to release anything that causes stress or anxiety. It is also a good time to give thanks.

Crash Course on Meditation
What is Meditation?

Disclaimer: When I first began practicing meditation, it had nothing to do with Jesus.

I did breath-counting, focused breathing, mantras, sound meditation, and different forms of transcendental meditation. After six years of practicing, I finally incorporated God by repeating the phrase *I am*. Two years later, I specifically used the name of Jesus. My soul now has rest, a deeper relationship with God, great friends and family. I live a richer, more full, abundant life by God's grace. However, the practice at its true essence is a tool that can and will help us worship the Lord.

When we close our eyes and repeat Jesus in our minds, we are doing more than just repeating a mantra. We are saying the name of the physical manifestation of God, who lived on earth. He was the only perfect being to ever live on earth. By focusing our mind on repeating the perfect name of Jesus, we are doing many things to enrich our lives all at once.

When we mediate and repeat the name of Jesus we are doing the following:

1. Actively submitting our full being to God-mind, body, and spirit.
2. Putting every thought, feeling, and emotion that arises beneath Jesus.
3. Making time for the Holy Spirit who is always with us as a helper.
4. Putting the past and future in the hands of Jesus.
5. Understanding that our physical inaction is trusting that God will open doors, direct our paths, put the right people in our lives, and work things out in a way that we may not see or understand immediately.

6. Allowing our time, actions, and thoughts not to be our governors.
7. Giving ourselves access to peace, rest, and freedom is available right now.
8. Facing the guilt, shame, fear, temptation, doubt, discouragement, true motives, imperfections, negative thought patterns, and our truest thoughts are about our own selves. Despite all the "ugly" parts of ourselves, we realize that God still loves us fully and wants us to seek Him. All this leads to seeing how truly perfect Jesus is, which helps us understand why we need a savior.

By God's grace, you might see a vision, hear something spiritual, reveal wisdom, receive guidance, or feel the presence of God. The point, however, is not to achieve these things. We meditate as a means to slow down from our lives, physically, stop, and move closer to God. Reading the bible before meditation helps tremendously. By slowing down and focusing our minds on Jesus, we are giving ourselves the chance to be fully human, embrace our flaws, learn more about ourselves, align our desires with Christ, and not be controlled by the physical world around us. We also see what things are on our minds that we need to pray for or give to God. This leads to a life where we can openly experience our full range of emotions. No piece of your being gets denied, and there is no need to try and be perfect. Just be yourself. Living a life like this helps you manage stress better, reduce anxiety, and worry less about life.

By meditating in this fashion, reading the gospel, and doing our best to live a life like Jesus (knowing we will fall short), we gain a different perspective. This will allow us to move about life in a more compassionate, joyful, loving, peaceful way, while still having boundaries, which ultimately will be felt by those we encounter. Creating undisturbed time for the Lord is the most valuable thing we could give Him and a sacrifice that is based out of love.

How to Meditate

I have found that the best way to meditate is to combine breathing techniques and mantras (repeating a word or phrase). Using these two things as a way to focus the Lord becomes truly transformative, not only as you meditate, but also throughout your day.

Before beginning a meditation, I recommend praying to God. Acknowledge his majesty, give thanks, and be vulnerable. Tell God what is troubling you and how you need his help.

Step 1: Sit in a comfortable position that you can remain in during the entire meditation.

Step 2: Set a timer for how long you would like to meditate. Start small.

Step 3: Gently close your eyes.

Step 4: Anytime you breathe in, mentally repeat "Abba." (ah-bah)

Step 5: Anytime you breathe out, mentally repeat "Jesus."

Step 6: Repeat these steps until the timer runs out.

Step 7: Thank God for giving you the time to sit and be still.

Additional Notes:

- Reading the Bible, listening to sermon, doing a devotion, or listening to worship music prior to meditation can help further focus your mind on the Lord.
- If you would like to repeat any other name of God, you are welcome to do so. For me, these two

names have been transformative.

- As you continue to practice meditation, the names of God will be continually on your mind because they are connected to your breath. Every breath is an acknowledgement of our creator, savior, and redeemer.
- If your mind begins to wander, it's okay. Simply return to your breath and the name of God.
- Don't feel bad if you need to itch, move, or readjust yourself. The point is not to idolize stillness but rather to return your mind continually to Jesus.

1 Corinthians 12:7–8 (ESV) - To each is given the manifestation of the Spirit for the common good. For to one is given through the Spirit the utterance of wisdom, and to another the utterance of knowledge according to the same Spirit.

These things have been revealed to me by the grace of God through Jesus. It is my duty to share what knowledge the spirit has freely given me.

The Goal of Meditation

The goal of meditation from a Christ centered point
of view is passive something and active nothing at the
same time. Don't seek knowledge. Don't seek wisdom.
Don't seek visions. Don't seek spiritual encounters.
Don't seek to be enlightened. Instead, by the grace of
God, allow yourself to receive all of these things and
much more beyond your own expectations. Let God
reveal himself. He is the center, not you.

This form of meditation is not meant to empty
your mind or the self. Instead, it is to fill yourself and
your mind with richness and glory. Meditation for any
amount of time is like choosing to have daily sabbath.
Sow your sabbath seed every morning and receive rest,
prosperity, and a fresh perspective from the Lord.

More than Meditation

The Lord wants us to live life as fully as possible, not
just sit around and do nothing. Meditation is a tool used
to relax and focus our minds on the Lord. Instead of
meditation being a tool to serve the Lord, meditation
itself can become an idol.

We were created to do so much more than just sit
still. Go have a good time, laugh, cry, spend times with
loved ones, be curious, love others, embrace getting hurt
emotionally, work toward your goals, sing along to the
song, dance to the music, learn about what interested
you, enjoy entertainment, listen to other people's stories,
take care of your animals, create something awesome,
overcome difficulties, build bonds, cook a beautiful
meal, take a walk, mend a fractured relationship, and
take a nap. There is so much to do in this world

Meditate, but do not forsake the wonders of all it
means to be human; to experience all it means to have
an abundant life. Being still is a small part of serving the

Lord, a tiny but meaningful part of living, and a little portion of all it means to be human.

On the 8th hour of "restoration three," during a two-hour mediation, I came to this realization. Your cup will never be filled by emptying yourself.

I personally believe that meditating for an hour in the morning after reading the Bible and praying before starting your day is more than enough. Meditation should not be done out of escapism, not wanting to deal with life, seeking meaning or searching for God.

Meaning is everywhere. God has already revealed Himself through the Bible and Jesus and will continue to reveal Himself to you with your eyes opened or closed at any place, at any time. Don't spend so much time doing nothing that you disrespect everything.

I don't search for my identity through meditation. My identity is found only in the Lord, God Almighty, through the grace of Jesus Christ.

A Simple but Peaceful Way to Live

As you get further along meditating, it impacts how you live your life when your eyes are open, and you are not seated. You begin to want to do nothing that distracts you from focusing. In my case, since my mantras are "Abba" and "Jesus," anything I do that is not in line with my faith is clearer in the moment. Then when I sit for meditation with whatever I did "wrong" is at the forefront of my mind. I am more mindful of my actions, thoughts, and words. When I do say or do the wrong thing, I feel horrible. Being mindful of what is wrong makes doing those things hurt even more.

Living a life in line with what Jesus taught, praying for forgiveness and things out of your control, and giving thanks, makes meditation much easier. I have become more aware of what I allow myself to listen to or watch. What a person consumes in some shape or form has power over them and on them. Unintentionally throughout the day, I also breathe in and repeat" Abba" and breathe out and repeat "Jesus" in my mind without trying to. This brings awareness to my thoughts, actions, and speech, which brings awareness to if I am living a life pleasing to Jesus. Mediation has made me begin to pray so much more because I realized all the things I can't change, even about my own self. Prayer is a part of meditation, enhances meditation, and is best used to complement one another.

After a few years of living out this format myself, I can guarantee the full collection of these things will bring you a sense of joy, peace of mind, content, and love, which in the end will lead to a much richer life. Make time for the Lord and always find reasons to be thankful. Love your family and cherish your friends. Pray for others. Remain kind and accept others no matter how difficult it may appear to be. At the end of the day, we are all the same, so refuse to compare.

Spend time in nature, eat mindfully, drink water, and move your body. Live as slowly as possible and lose yourself in as many moments as possible. Do your best and enjoy what it is. Finally, continue to laugh and smile because life will be life.

Part I: Conception

"This is where it begins."

Opening Prayer

This is the day the Lord has made. I will rejoice and be glad.

Thank You for Your unfailing love and wonderful deeds.

You are my strength and my shield. My heart trusts in You.

Because You care for me, I cast all of my stress and anxiety on to You.

Allow me to give thanks to You, in all circumstances, because all things will pass.

Help me not to lean on my own understanding and instead keep my mind in Your perfect peace.

Your ways are higher than my ways. Your thoughts are higher than my thoughts.

Through Your love, allow me to be loving, gentle, kind, patient, and to show self-control.

Help me to accept others as Christ accepts me.

Lord, please humble me, direct my path, shower me with confidence, bless me with perseverance, and help me make the most of my short time on earth.

Amen.

This personal prayer is a combination of multiple Bible verses including the following: Psalm 118:24, Psalm 107:8, Psalm 28:7, 1 Peter 5:7, 1 Thessalonians 5:18, Mark 10:27, Philippians 4:13, Psalm 90:14, Philippians 4:4, Proverbs 3:5, Romans 3:23, Isaiah 26:3, Romans 12:18, Galatians 5:13, Luke 6:38, Galatians 5:22-23, Romans 15:7, Proverbs 3:6, James 4:10,, Philippians 1:6, James 1:12, Ephesians 5:15-16, Psalm 90:12

Until I

Until I went outside, I couldn't smell the flowers.

Until I looked an animal in the eyes, I didn't know my
ignorance.

Until I lost everything, I didn't realize I was nothing.

Meditation I

Thank You, Lord, for answering the prayers of my heart. You are truly God alone. You are God not because of what You do but because You are God.

In my times of trouble, sadness, and uncertainty, You were all I had. You were the only one I could turn to. You were the only one who could understand. You were the only one who could bring change. You were the only one who could save me from the disappointment of this world.

Thank You for answering my prayers in visible ways that remind me You are orchestrating everything. I can only give thanks and praise for You allowing things to work in my favor, even though I was, and still am, undeserving.

Thank You for Your mercy. You turned my tears of sadness into tears of joy. You turned my anxiety to present rest. You turned my worry into present peace.

In Your goodness, You have changed my life, which is more than I asked for. You let me be more childlike. You helped me let go of useless philosophy, and You allowed me to simply enjoy.

You have given me a better relationship with my family, a woman I adore, friends I cherish deeply, and a life full of more avenues to success than I originally asked for.

Help me not to so quickly forget Your marvelous deeds. Help me to always give thanks for what You have blessed me with, even when it's challenging.

By Your grace, do I write these words. By Your kindness can I look back and see Your hand in all things done to me, for me, and around me.

Lord, allow me to remember as long as I live that You are a God who answers prayers. You have provided for me greater than I could have imagined and in ways I could not see or understand at first.

Allow me to have confidence that You will do the same again and again because You are God, and I trust in You. You allow my testimony of the past to increase my present faith in You.

By God's grace, through our Lord Jesus, Amen.

Blooming

There was once a magnificent flower that wanted to be a tree.

He prayed and prayed and prayed that the Lord would allow him to turn into a tree.

The Lord tested the flower and made it start to lose its beautiful petals. The flower cried and prayed again to the Lord.

"Wait! I don't want to be a tree if it means losing my wonderful petals!"

Little did the flower know that it was the time of year when he always loses his petals.

Dog Story

One day, my dog, Keiko, ran away. I let her out to use the bathroom, and she raced into the woods. I knew what was happening and yelled out, but she was off. I screamed her name over and over again, but I had to take more action. I searched for her on foot for what felt like hours. I became angry. I ran home to get my car; I drove around awhile and still couldn't find her. I accepted that she was gone. My anger turned to sadness. I imagined the danger she could be in. I returned home, went to the backyard, and looked up to the Lord. I gave thanks for the experience of owning a dog. I took a deep breath and turned to go inside when Keiko sprinted toward me, jumping for joy. I picked her up, hugged her, and said, "thank you for coming back. I'm so glad you're safe." And she blinked.

How much more will the Lord seek us out? How much more compassion does He have for us? How much more does the Lord embrace us when we return? How much more ignorant are we as people, not knowing that we are lost but finding joy when we return to the Lord?

Distractions

We are born sinners and our minds & the enemy does not want us to focus our full attention on the Lord. Despite the distractions that arise, no matter how repetitive, we must continue to focus our mind repeating the Lord's name. His name is Jesus. His name is above all names, and he has authority over all things, including our thoughts. Meditation, done with Christ at the center, is a practical form of making all thoughts captive and submitting your full being to Jesus. Filling our minds with scripture and hiding it in our hearts will lead us to having power over those thoughts as they arise because the truth will set us free from their power.

Biblical References

Philippians 2:9 (ESV) – Therefore God has highly exalted him and bestowed on him the name that is above every name.

Matthew 28:18 (ESV) – And Jesus came and said to them, "All authority in heaven and on earth has been given to me."

2 Corinthians 10:5 (ESV) – We destroy arguments and every lofty opinion raised against the knowledge of God and take every thought captive to obey Christ.

James 4:7 (ESV) – Submit yourselves therefore to God. Resist the devil, and he will flee from you.

Psalm 119:11 (ESV) – I have stored up your word in my heart, that I might not sin against you.

John 8:32 (ESV) – And you will know the truth, and the truth will set you free.

Boredom

Our minds & the enemy want us to do everything but stop and be still. There are so many things we must do in our lives, so much to think about, plans we need to make, people we need to spend time with, and responsibilities that we have to do. Does God not know all these things?

Are you willing to submit your full being to God, physically, emotionally, mentally, and spiritually, finding rest that He has complete control over all parts of your life? You will exchange boredom for peace, have greater trust in the Lord, and find rest in His presence. Will all the things that God blessed you with keep you away from Him? Will the pace of life shake you from your foundation? Find time for stillness and silence.

Boredom, in many ways, is the door to experiencing Christ in a way you never have before. In the past, God resided in a physical temple in Jerusalem. Now, we, ourselves, are the temple of God.

Biblical References

Psalm 46:10 (ESV) – Be still, and know that I am God. I will be exalted among the nations, I will be exalted in the earth!

1 John 3:20 (ESV) – For whenever our heart condemns us, God is greater than our heart, and he knows everything.

Psalm 139:4 (ESV) – Even before a word is on my tongue, behold, O Lord, you know it altogether.

James 4:7 (ESV) – Submit yourselves therefore to God. Resist the devil, and he will flee from you.

Mark 6:31 (ESV) – And he said to them, "Come away by yourselves to a desolate place and rest a while."

Romans 1:25 (ESV) – Because they exchanged the truth about God for a lie and worshiped and served the creature rather than the Creator, who is blessed forever! Amen.

Matthew 7:24–25 (ESV) – Everyone then who hears these words of mine and does them will be like a wise man who built his house on the rock. And the rain fell, and the floods came, and the winds blew and beat on that house, but it did not fall, because it had been founded on the rock.

1 Corinthians 3:16 (ESV) – Do you not know that you are God's temple and that God's Spirit dwells in you?

Lamentations 3:28 (ESV) – Let him sit alone in silence when it is laid on Him.

Zephaniah 1:7 (ESV) – Be silent before the Lord God! For the day of the Lord is near.

Part 2: Reflection

"Live intentionally,
mindful, yet freely."

Opening Prayer

Thank You, Lord, for placing eternity in my heart.

Thank You for the Holy Spirit's presence as I seek You.

Thank You, Lord, for this time to meditate.

Thank You for allowing me to sit still, be still, and know that You are God.

May Your peace that surpasses all understanding guard my heart and my mind as I meditate.

Whenever my mind wanders, may You refocus my mind on Your holy name and on the Kingdom which is within me.

May You reveal Your glory to me as I meditate.

In Jesus's name, Amen.

By

Live life by progress

Live life by learning

Live life by gratefulness

Live life purposefully

Then, do it all over again, knowing that Your life is written by God.

Love is

Love does not seek to change; love appreciates.

Love is not self serving; love is selfless.

Love is not conditional; love is continual.

Love has no expectation; love embraces.

Love is not emotionless; love is vulnerable.

Meditation II

Thanks be to our ever-present God who exists now, forever, and always.

I am grateful to serve a God who is so complex but truly simple in nature… a simplicity far beyond my own understanding.

I am imperfect, evil by nature, and proud from birth. Yet, God's grace and mercy shower over me.

A drop of Your presence is more intoxicating than anything the earth has to offer.

A moment with You is more addictive than any vice.

In my confusion, misunderstanding, and doubt, Your presence brings me clarity, joy, and rest.

I will turn my eyes to You, always.

In good, bad, happy, sad, peaceful, and stressful times, I will turn my eyes to You, always.

Keep my needs short; provide the things You desire for me so I may direct attention to You

now and for all the days I live on earth, by Your grace.

Amen.

Don't Make it Make Sense

The Rich Man

In one city where I lived for work, there was once a man who impacted me more than almost any other man who worked in the building. At first, he was a bit quiet and shy, but over the course of a few months, we became friends, and we would spend long periods of time talking.

He was kind, willing to be vulnerable, shared things he had been through, admitted his flaws, gave advice, told me about friends and family, asked me questions, listened, and he genuinely wanted the best for me and my future.

This man had dropped out of school, been to jail, and was now a janitor. He couldn't give me or get me anything I couldn't get on my own. He wasn't the richest person in the building. He wasn't truly known by many. He was well-intentioned, thoughtful, reflective, and thankful to be in the building and have his job.

Sometimes people would walk in the room while we were speaking, and he would get quiet, stop talking, or even leave the room. He gave into his place, "status" or "role," society and the building gave him.

It made my soul sad. The "bad" decisions he made in the past, his current job, issues he was struggling with, and his present problems did not define who he truly was at the core. He is a creation of God who Christ died for. Regardless of the physical problems people could point out, he, I, and everyone else in the building are all completely equal.

Jesus loves the broken, the needy, the rejected, the oppressed, the poor, and those who were wrong doers because they are willing to share how much they need help and can't rely on themselves. The rich, famous, or those with status can mask their problems, but the root of the problem will always remain.

Comparison/Jealousy/Coveting

Our minds & the enemy want you to judge others and desire everything you don't have, especially when you see others possess it. Our minds/the enemy want you to believe that someone else's life or what they have is better than what we have, which ultimately demeans our personal blessings. The Lord has a plan, purpose, and reason for all people, including you. He has given you exactly what you need and is withholding nothing good from you. Appreciate what other people have without taking away from who you are, what you think you lack, your blessings, and what the Lord is doing in your own life. Be as joyful for others as you are for yourself.

Biblical References

Esther 4:14 (ESV) – For if you keep silent at this time, relief and deliverance will rise for the Jews from another place, but you and your father's house will perish. And who knows whether you have not come to the kingdom for such a time as this?

James 3:16 (ESV) – For where jealousy and selfish ambition exist, there will be disorder and every vile practice.

Galatians 6:4 (ESV) – But let each one test his own work, and then his reason to boast will be in himself alone and not in his neighbor.

Exodus 20:17 (ESV) – You shall not covet your neighbor's house; you shall not covet your neighbor's wife, or his male servant, or his female servant, or his ox, or his donkey, or anything that is your neighbor's.

Hebrews 4:15 (ESV) – For we do not have a high priest who is unable to sympathize with our weaknesses, but one who in every respect has been tempted as we are, yet without sin.

Obsessive Nostalgia

Our minds & the enemy wants you to focus on the past more than the present in an unhealthy way. Our mind/ the enemy wants you to be convinced that old things, old times, and old people are better than what God has blessed with you now, in this moment. The Lord has placed you where you are, around certain people, living your exact life because He needs you here right now. Appreciate and give thanks for the past without letting it damage the gift of the present.

Biblical References

Ecclesiastes 7:10 (ESV) – Say not, "Why were the former days better than these?" For it is not from wisdom that you ask this.

Isaiah 43:18 (ESV) – Remember not the former things, nor consider the things of old.

Part 3: Expectation

"Don't let your desires ruin your experience."

Opening Prayer

You Lord, our God, are far better than I could have ever imagined.

Devotion to You is beyond infinity. Worshiping You is eternal.

You are phenomenally good, other worldly amazing, and far beyond the limitation of my thoughts.

You, Lord, our God, are the Source of all creation, the Light to all things, and Your Presence is in all places, even when unfelt.

Thank You that I may know You and experience You, even if it is a fraction of a fraction of Your fullness.

Amen.

The Vine

Your rhythm is divine,
Your love is sacred.

You remind me I'm fine,
Even when I am shaken.

In my darkness You shine,
All my sins are taken.

You are the True Vine,
Forever my firm foundation.

The Fish

Greg believes fish can only survive in the water.

Owen believes fish are watching us.

Daisy believes fish are stupid.

Ian believes fish are the creators of the sea.

Sam believes fish tastes really good.

Hallie believes fish are scary.

Ed believes fish are a creation of God.

Raul believes fish eventually turn into mammals

Ellie believes fish are not real but only live in her mind.

Ned believes fish are part of the food chain.

Ollie believes fish are warm-blooded.

Winnie believes fish are not important.

Today, every single one of these people had to put on a jacket because it was snowing. No matter if a person believes in the truth, part of the truth, none of the truth, or a lie, the truth still exists. Each person must still face what it means to be human.

Meditation III

My God, My God, I will never truly know You or completely understand You in this life. You reveal Yourself at times and give signs, but You are so far above me. What You reveal or show is merely a glimpse of who You are. Forgive me if my mind tries to reduce you to less. You are unfathomable. I pray You allow me to experience Your fullness as I seek You and fellowship with others, through Jesus.

In this life, I have faced pain, suffering, and discouragement that few people know the extent of. God, Your presence, is with me now and You are ever present. You are the source of ultimate joy. You want us to cry out to You, be vulnerable, and lift our voices to You-even more so in times of trouble. You, God, who hears all things, comfort me, bring me rest, and continue to change my life in unimaginable ways.

I will lift up my voice and pray to You, Lord. Mediation without prayer is like making food without eating it. Sitting in silence is a part but not the full scope of serving You. I will continually bring my burdens to Your feet. My pain and suffering will always be before You. I know as Your servant that I will always find rest knowing that You hear me, You listen, and You are always with me.

Thank You for destroying hopelessness and giving me courage to fight. My destiny is in Your hands, Lord. Amen.

The Father Story

There was once a father with five children. The oldest child lied often. As the child grew up, they began to realize their father was a liar. Not only could they not trust their father, but they couldn't trust God or His promises. The second child never spent time with their father unless the dad thought they were doing well enough in school. As that child grew, they felt they had to be perfect. Unfortunately, it led to the child rejecting God because they felt they could never be good enough. The middle child was constantly beaten by their father.

As they grew up, they feared God, became overly religious, didn't embrace their humanity, and couldn't begin to understand how much God loved them. The fourth child was given away at birth because the father felt he already had too many kids. That child not only felt abandoned by their father, but also by God, and could never fully embrace relying on God. The father felt so terrible about what happened to the fourth child that he decided to be the best father he could be for the next child.

He loved them fully, allowed them to be themselves, and disciplined them when appropriate. He was there for them, helped them toward their dreams, and provided everything that he could. That child grew to love God, have a strong faith, and maintain a beautiful relationship with the Heavenly Father. Fathers, be cautious of how you raise children. Earthly fathers are the first example to a young person of what God is like. Though every earthly father will fall short, everyone blessed to have children should give them a glimpse of how much greater God the Father is for all of us who believe.

Paradise was never a physical place, but a place of mind.

Issues/Problems

Our minds & the enemy want you to think about all that can be better, different, or change. However, nothing happens that the Lord does not know about or does not allow. As hard as it may be, give thanks in all circumstances. Sometimes, the things we don't want cause suffering. However, suffering produces endurance, endurance produces character, and character produces hope. All things will shape us into who God most desires us to be. His will be done instead of ours.

Biblical References

Psalm 139:16 (ESV) – Your eyes saw my unformed substance; in your book were written, every one of them, the days that were formed for me, when as yet there was none of them.

Lamentations 3:37 (ESV) – Who has spoken, and it came to pass, unless the Lord has commanded it?

1 Thessalonians 5:18 (ESV) – Give thanks in all circumstances; for this is the will of God in Christ Jesus for you.

Job 2:10 (ESV) – But he said to her, "You speak as one of the foolish women would speak. Shall we receive good from God, and shall we not receive evil?" In all this Job did not sin with his lips.

Ephesians 2:10 (ESV) – For we are his workmanship, created in Christ Jesus for good works, which God prepared beforehand, that we should walk in them.

Isaiah 64:8 (ESV) – But now, O Lord, you are our Father; we are the clay, and you are our potter; we are all the work of your hand.

Matthew 6:10 (ESV) – Your kingdom come, your will be done, on earth as it is in heaven.

Luke 22:42 (ESV) – Saying, "Father, if you are willing, remove this cup from me. Nevertheless, not my will, but yours, be done."

Job 23:14 (ESV) – For he will complete what he appoints for me, and many such things are in his mind.

Worry/Fear/ Anxiety

Our minds & the enemy want you to be concerned about the future, think of the worst outcomes, and desire control that is not meant to be yours. The Lord knows beginning to end, comforts us in times of need, and is in perfect control. The Lord wants you to look at Him alone, not your circumstance, good or bad.

Biblical References

Matthew 6:34 (ESV) – Therefore do not be anxious about tomorrow, for tomorrow will be anxious for itself. Sufficient for the day is its own trouble.

Proverbs 19:21 (ESV) – Many are the plans in the mind of a man, but it is the purpose of the Lord that will stand.

Matthew 11:28–30 (ESV) – Come to me, all who labor and are heavy laden, and I will give you rest. Take my yoke upon you, and learn from me, for I am gentle and lowly in heart, and you will find rest for your souls. For my yoke is easy, and my burden is light.

Isaiah 40:23 (ESV) – Who brings princes to nothing and makes the rulers of the earth as emptiness.

Isaiah 46:9–10 (ESV) – Remember the former things of old; for I am God, and there is no other; I am God, and there is none like me, declaring the end from the beginning and from ancient times things not yet done, saying, "My counsel shall stand, and I will accomplish all my purpose."

Isaiah 49:13 (ESV) – Sing for joy, O heavens, and exult, O earth; break forth, O mountains, into singing! For the Lord has comforted his people and will have compassion on his afflicted.

Philippians 4:6 (ESV) – Do not be anxious about anything, but in everything by prayer and supplication with thanksgiving let your requests be made known to God.

Luke 12:25–26 (ESV) – And which of you by being anxious can add a single hour to his span of life? If then you are not able to do as small a thing as that, why are you anxious about the rest?

Joshua 1:9 (ESV) – Have I not commanded you? Be strong and courageous. Do not be frightened, and do not be dismayed, for the Lord your God is with you wherever you go.

Deuteronomy 31:6 (ESV) – Be strong and courageous. Do not fear or be in dread of them, for it is the Lord your God who goes with you. He will not leave you or forsake you.

Jeremiah 29:11 (ESV) – For I know the plans I have for you, declares the Lord, plans for welfare and not for evil, to give you a future and a hope.

Part 4: Adoration

"Love will move you
forward."

Opening Prayer

You created everything I can see,

From the birds and bees,

To the grass and the trees,

From the sky to the ground,

 You too, created light and sound.

Your creation reveals Your majesty,

Order in each and every place,

 Intention behind every beautiful face,

You are Lord of every age,

You too, are the God of all faith and grace.

Who may know You but those who seek You,

Who may seek You but those who You reveal.

Oh, how You love your creation that we may love You,

Oh, how worthy You are of every kneel,

You too, are the God who Heals.

The More I Wanted

The more I wanted God, the less I cared about what He could do for me.

The less I wanted, the more God provided.

Behind Those Eyes

Behind those eyes, there is peace, joy, and love.

Behind those eyes, the *creator* is here and above.

Behind those eyes, His spirit rests like a dove.

Behind those eyes, feel the warm embrace of a Heavenly hug.

You Breathed

You breathed into all people the breath of life.

With every breath in, I will acknowledge the creator, and with every breath out, I will acknowledge the savior, with the help of the helper. You are the same God.

You command me to come with You by myself to a quiet place and get some rest. Here I am Lord. In my solitude, I desire Your still, small voice. When I am still, You move. In my inaction, You are active. In my inability, You are able. When I am quiet, Your voice is made clear. In my silence, You comfort me. When I am mute, Your majesty is undeniable.

When my eyes are closed, Your eyes are open to all things. When my eyes are shut, You guide me through the darkness. When my eyes rest, You are there.

Perfectly Good

God is the only thing that does not come with extra problems. He is perfectly good. I need nothing else. I want nothing else. Anything I have become is never as cool as I thought it would be before I became it. Everything I wanted comes with its own set of problems or issues that I couldn't have known about until I got it. God remains consistent-no drawbacks, my safe haven, worth the time and energy, and perfectly good. He is enough.

You are the same in my clarity.

You are the same in my happiness.

You are the same in my peace.

You are the same in my joy.

You are the same when I am not.

You are the same in my confusion.

You are the same in my sadness.

You are the same in my anxiety.

You are the same in my stress.

Thank You for always being the same.

Meditation IV

Thank You, heavenly Father, for everything.

Thank You, Lord Jesus, for laying Your life for all the world.

Thank You for hearing my voice, though I am merely a man.

What can happen that You don't know about?

What has happened that You did not allow?

What can I experience that You don't understand?

What thoughts can I hide from You Lord?

What can I do that You cannot?

Thank You, Lord, for Your ever-present nature that never fails me. At times, I think bad thoughts, do the wrong thing, and seek to please myself, yet Your mercy is continual. At times, I am selfish, prideful, and worried about the future, but Your love never turns away from me. Ashamed of who I once was, You always urge me to focus on who You have allowed me to become.

Thank You, Lord, for Your ever-present nature that never fails me. Loneliness tries to eat away at my mind. Pointlessness weighs my body down. Lord, free me from all chains, even if I am the one who put them on in the first place. If anything has a grip on me, Lord, let it be Your grip alone. I have done so little, yet, You have blessed me so much. You have shown me the security of my future but have kept the pathway from me. Lord, give me the peace of mind that You will take care of all things, to come, and I can remain present. Help me to be more focused on You instead of the circumstances in front of me, good, bad, or in between. Every pain, issue, or problem brings me closer to You Lord. What a blessing!

Keep my heart humble no matter the things You allow me to gain. Keep my mind focused on You no matter the thoughts that arise. Lord, help me to forgive cheerfully and hold no grudges. Lord, please keep my mind from perfectionism, and keep my heart from being over righteous. Give me the peace of mind to always persevere and rely on You as my source of strength. In the end, I am but a man, nothing without You, Lord Jesus. Through You, I am a child of God and a sheep of the Good Shepherd, my only true identity. Thank You for loving me long before I ever realized it. I love You Lord. Amen.

The Fly Story

There was once a fly named Steven. His life expectancy was thirty-one days. He lived in a dumpster truck, but he had a dream to taste the most expensive, delicious steak in the world. He flew out of the dumpster truck leaving his family and friends behind. For three days, he flew through traffic without stopping. Finally, he arrived at a random family's house and rested until the seventh day. On the eighth day, the family grilled steak. He tasted it and knew there was some better out there to try. He waited around to see if they would grill again, but they did not. On the twelfth day, he left. He traveled for six days and arrived at a mansion on the eighteenth day. The family prepared steaks on the nineteenth day. It was the most amazing thing he had ever tried, but he still believed there was better. Instead of going home, he left to go to the best restaurant in the city. He arrived on the twenty-fourth day and slept through the night. On the twenty-fifth day, the most expensive steak in the world was wheeled out to the table for a family of four celebrating a birthday. Steven landed on the steak. It tasted amazing, but the steak was so hot, it killed him. None of the flies know who he is, but now you do.

Blessed When Serving Others

We are truly blessed when we serve others, listen to one another, sacrifice for each other, encourage a friend, share our belongings, give freely, forgive those who are wrong to us, have compassion for people struggling, are willing to apologize no matter how small the offense, pray with others, pray for others, and extend kindness to strangers.

The Girl of my Dreams: A True Story

One day, while sitting across a room, I saw the most beautiful woman I had ever seen. It wasn't the kind of beauty I was used to. This was different, something I was experiencing for the first time. She shined. Her presence was strong yet calm. She was quiet and peaceful, but unmistakably there. Her pure being was captivating.

She didn't notice me. Or maybe she just didn't know I existed. Either way, I couldn't stop thinking about her.

A few nights later, she appeared in my dream. We were having a conversation in my mom's old room, now empty except for a bed and a vanity. Someone walked in the room in the middle of our deep chat, but I immediately made them leave. My attention was entirely on her mind, body, and spirit.

I woke up and brushed it off. A dream is just a dream, I thought.

Weeks passed. One day, I found myself praying. I told God that I wanted to deepen my faith, to draw closer to Him, and to rely on Him alone. The next day, coincidentally, I was baptized.

That night, she appeared again in my dreams. This time, I was walking down the steps of my house. She was waiting by the couch. I asked her what she was doing there. She replied gently, "Waiting for you." I woke up, and I knew it was God.

The next day, in real life, she walked past me in a lobby. Just her and me. She glanced, smiled, this warm, heart-melting smile, and said, "hi." I said, "hey." And just like that, she was gone.

Over the next three days, I asked around to see if

anyone knew whether she was in a relationship or not. Everyone said yes. I was disappointed, but I accepted it. That was reality.

Then strangely, that night, there she was in one of my dreams again.

In this dream, she and I, along with a few people we both knew, were at a party. I walked straight up to her and asked if she was seeing anyone. She laughed and said, "No, but I've been waiting for you to speak to me." I smiled, and we talked. And talked. And talked.

Afterward, we left the party and went for a drive. She drove. I sat beside her. We talked, laughed, and shared stories. She dropped me off in front of a beautiful hotel, smiled, and though she didn't say a word, I knew she'd be back. And then I woke up.

That morning, I prayed, "Lord, the next time I see her one-on-one, I'll speak to her if it's your will."

A week passed. I didn't see her.

Another week passed, and I ran into her while walking with a friend down a hallway. She happened to be stepping into an elevator. I sprinted down the stairs hoping to catch her. But by the time I got to the bottom, she was gone. I was disappointed, but then I remembered my prayer was to see her one-on-one.

Two days later, it happened. I naturally ran into her alone. Just the two of us. She smiled and said "hi" in a playful, joking way. I knew it was time. We spoke, and that night, we went on our first date. It was perfect.

This woman has one of the strongest faiths I've ever known. Her testimony is powerful. Her life is devoted to pleasing God. She's changed me. She's helped me deepen my faith and trust in God more fully in a way I thought could only happen by myself. She is the most precious gift God has ever given me.

God answers prayers in ways we don't always see or understand. Sometimes, He speaks through dreams. Who I am now would be impossible without God and without experiencing Him through this woman.

Pride

Our minds & the enemy want you to see yourself, your circumstances, and your life from your own perspective and standards. Living a life like this is only pleasing to self. Without God, we are worthless, senseless, and foolish. Fix your mind on the Lord's standard, truth, and expectations for us instead.

Biblical References

Galatians 1:10 (ESV) – For am I now seeking the approval of man, or of God? Or am I trying to please man? If I were still trying to please man, I would not be a servant of Christ.

Proverbs 3:5–6 (ESV) – Trust in the Lord with all your heart, and do not lean on your own understanding. In all your ways acknowledge him, and he will make straight your paths.

Jeremiah 10:23 (ESV) – I know, O Lord, that the way of man is not in himself, that it is not in man who walks to direct his steps.

Colossians 3:2 (ESV) – Set your minds on things that are above, not on things that are on earth.

Philippians 4:8 (ESV) – Finally, brothers, whatever is true, whatever is honorable, whatever is just, whatever is pure, whatever is lovely, whatever is commendable, if there is any excellence, if there is anything worthy of praise, think about these things.

Psalm 119:137–138 (ESV) – Righteous are you, O Lord, and right are your rules. You have appointed your testimonies in righteousness and in all faithfulness.

1 John 2:16–17 (ESV) – For all that is in the world—the

desires of the flesh and the desires of the eyes and pride in possessions—is not from the Father but is from the world. And the world is passing away along with its desires, but whoever does the will of God abides forever.

Jeremiah 9:23 (ESV) – Thus says the Lord: "Let not the wise man boast in his wisdom, let not the mighty man boast in his might, let not the rich man boast in his riches."

Philippians 2:3 (ESV) – Do nothing from selfish ambition or conceit, but in humility count others more significant than yourselves.

Romans 1:28 (ESV) – And since they did not see fit to acknowledge God, God gave them up to a debased mind to do what ought not to be done.

Regret/Shame/Guilt

Our minds & the enemy want us to focus on what you did wrong or said wrong. All your worst mistakes and everything you could have done differently in the past. By extension, our mind or the enemy will try to make you feel disappointed in who you are and want you to think less of yourself. However, remember, you will never be perfect, nor do you need to be. This Lord's grace is sufficient and his blood covers all wrongdoing. Nothing, including, what you have done can separate you from the love of God. You are well made, completely known, accepted, forgiven, and loved. From this view, we should never even judge ourselves.

Biblical References

Psalm 18:30 (ESV) – This God—his way is perfect; the word of the Lord proves true; he is a shield for all those who take refuge in him.

2 Corinthians 12:9 (ESV) – But he said to me, "My grace is sufficient for you, for my power is made perfect in weakness." Therefore, I will boast all the more gladly of my weaknesses, so that the power of Christ may rest upon me.

1 John 1:7 (ESV) – But if we walk in the light, as he is in the light, we have fellowship with one another, and the blood of Jesus his Son cleanses us from all sin.

Romans 8:39 (ESV) – Nor height nor depth, nor anything else in all creation, will be able to separate us from the love of God in Christ Jesus our Lord.

1 Corinthians 4:3 (ESV) – But with me it is a very small thing that I should be judged by you or by any human court. In fact, I do not even judge myself.

Psalm 34:5 (ESV) – Those who look to him are radiant, and their faces shall never be ashamed.

Part 5:
Transformation

"Change is a choice."

Yahweh Tulay - A Small Prayer

You, Lord, have all the answers, even if You choose not to reveal them. You transcend all thoughts, languages, and spaces.

Tülay is a small fraction of describing You. Yet may I praise You, honor You, and glorify You, because You have given me this word.

You, Lord, Father, Son, and Spirit, are Tülay in every sense and beyond. You are gentle, elegant, majestic, and peaceful. You are my protector, my light in the darkness, and Your blood covers me. Your presence is soft, luminous, and powerful, all at once.

You have once again proven Yourself beyond comprehension, despite not needing to. May You allow me to remember You are Yahweh Tülay as long as I live.

Thank You, Lord.

Amen.

*If it is truly a message
from the Lord,
you'll know.*

G.M.I

Faithful prayer created your present joy.

Patience showed you the way.

You will smile forever.

Slow is the New

The pace of life is meant to be slow.

The best deception is the one closest to the truth, beware.

I AM transcends all ways but is suitable for every way of life.

An old monkey can still make new faces.

Sprinter

Moving faster than a sprinter, we lose a fight we cannot
see.
Confusing and dark like winter, we toss and turn lost at
sea.

Choosing our outside determines our inner, we are
either a mayfly or tree.
Inducting ourselves as saint or sinner, we are who we are
meant to be

Meditation V

While meditating, I was thinking a lot, and then suddenly, this bright white light flashed beyond the darkness of my eyes. A light much brighter than the darkness of the room I was in as well. It scared me yet brought this sense of greater focus and peace. Then all of a sudden, my left foot began to strongly shake for a few seconds.

Then while sitting in the silence, all of the of things I was thinking of began to have immediate answers:

I had to give a speech soon and, in the silence, I was told to share my thoughts on how some people think faith is fake, even though it's real and the only thing that brings true peace. I was also to share how five years ago, what I wanted out of life would have led me to be selfish, self-centered, and lost. Who I ended up becoming was greater than I could have imagined. There is always possibility.

During my meditation I asked how to handle a long-distance relationship and I was prompted to "continue to love with steadfast love."

I asked where my next job would be and the immediate answer I got back was, "You'll know soon."

After this, I asked the Lord in my mind, "Show me a sign that shows this is You, not my own mind." I immediately heard back, "I already did."

Then I saw a vision of an older friend of mine, a blind man with a bad limp, walking perfectly and opening a door as if he could see. Then he held the door waiting for someone to walk in, but I didn't see anyone or anything in the doorframe.

I was back in the silence of meditation. Finally, while sitting there, I heard the word "too-leh" or "two-leh" and was prompted to find its meaning in Turkish. Then my meditation timer went off.

I immediately went to my phone and searched for that word in Turkish. The closest words that I could find was Tülay, a name meaning "as delicate as tulle and bright like the moon." A poetic way of describing someone as graceful and radiant. A Tulle is a light, fine, and airy fabric, describing a gentle, elegant, soft presence. The moon is majestic, peaceful, and light in darkness, describing radiant, calming, luminous presence. Together, this describes one who is both softly beautiful and quietly powerful-graceful in form, glowing in character. "A being soft in form, yet strong in presence."

This is astonishing to me because I know absolutely zero Turkish.

I did more research and found that it is a feminine name yet perfectly describes the Lord and my experience of Him in meditation and beyond. The Lord transcends gender in the way we think. From a spiritual sense, this perfectly embodies the characteristics of the Lord.

He is tender, compassionate, mysterious, transcendent—our cover, protector, light in the darkness. The Lord God is spirit, not male/female.

Isaiah 66:13 (ESV) – As one whom his mother comforts, so I will comfort you; you shall be comforted in Jerusalem.

All these things fit Jesus as well, confirming how He and the Spirit and the Father are one. He is gentle and compassionate, our light. While being beyond majestic, He chose humility by reducing himself to human being.

For the Lord, it is less of a name and more of an adjective or poetic description of the Great I AM. He embodies Tülay. His presence is Tülay. He is Tülay more than anyone could ever be.

The word in Turkish is pronounced more like "Two-Lie" but I am choosing to pronounce this word wrong, and to continue to pronounce it more like what I heard during meditation, Tūlay.

"They" Story/ Virgin Story

There was once a virgin. At seventeen years old, they prayed to God to be happily married by thirty-five. By twenty years old, they felt social pressure to be cool and be accepted. They were not proud of who they were, they had a desire to be connected to others, became addicted to pleasure, continually tried to fill a void by using others, compared themselves to all of their friends, and constantly needed approval from everyone, but God.

By age twenty-three, they had chosen over fifty sexual partners. Some they remember, and some they do not. Some were a mistake and some were not. Some were relationships, but most were not. Some were truly meaningful, but almost all were not. Some served a purpose, but in the end, none were worth it.

By twenty-nine, they were very isolated, lonely, insecure, selfish, hurt, damaged, anxious, entitled, transactional, spiteful, and weary of others. They decided to date around for a few years, but at age thirty-four, they gave up because they couldn't find the right person for several reasons. When they turned thirty-five, they were still single and angry at God. They prayed. *Why did You do this to me, God, I trusted in You!*

They stopped believing in God. Thoughts lead to sin. Sin leads to choices. Choices lead to a lifestyle that can damage our minds and hurt those around us. Don't blame God for what we chose to do. All of our choices impact who we become, who we spend time around, what happens to us. These choices that all begin as thoughts can affect a few people or many people. Don't blame God.

God loves us so much that He gives us the freedom

to not believe in Him, to reject Him, to turn away from Him, to rebel against Him, and to do whatever we choose. This love, at times, is above human understanding.

If God never gave you what you wanted, fixed your problems, answered your prayers, or changed the circumstances in your life you did not like, then who is God to you?

You have been a good friend to me. Thank you.

New Heights

To reach new heights, to experience growth, or to
become who we truly are, change is necessary. It can
be mental, physical, emotional, or spiritual. Change
will be uncomfortable to some degree. Through
acknowledgement, acceptance, and resting in the Lord,
we find that on the other side of being uncomfortable
lies peace and joy. A new perspective or a lesson that
could not have been learned otherwise. Thank the Lord
for His greater understanding.

Temptation

Our minds & the enemy want you to think about thoughts, memories, and fantasies that will entice you to sin. Be conscious of the fruits of the flesh. Resist the devil and his temptation, and he will flee from you. Know that these thoughts, memories, and fantasies come from the father of lies, who want you to stumble. Fill your mind with good things and focus more intentionally on the name of Jesus, the name above all names. Jesus has power over all things and has faced temptation himself. He will not let you get tempted more than you can handle.

Biblical References

Galatians 5:19–21 (ESV) – Now the works of the flesh are evident: sexual immorality, impurity, sensuality, idolatry, sorcery, enmity, strife, jealousy, fits of anger, rivalries, dissensions, divisions, envy, drunkenness, orgies, and things like these. I warn you, as I warned you before, that those who do such things will not inherit the kingdom of God.

James 4:7 (ESV) – Submit yourselves therefore to God. Resist the devil, and he will flee from you.

Philippians 4:8 (ESV) – Finally, brothers, whatever is true, whatever is honorable, whatever is just, whatever is pure, whatever is lovely, whatever is commendable, if there is any excellence, if there is anything worthy of praise, think about these things.

Matthew 4:1–11 (ESV) – Then Jesus was led up by the Spirit into the wilderness to be tempted by the devil. And after fasting forty days and forty nights, he was hungry. And the tempter came and said to him, "If you are the Son of God, command these stones to become loaves of bread." But he answered, "It is written, 'Man shall not live by bread alone, but by every word that comes from the mouth of God.'"

Then the devil took him to the holy city and set him on the pinnacle of the temple and said to him, "If you are the Son of God, throw yourself down, for it is written, 'He will command his angels concerning you,' and 'On their hands they will bear you up, lest you strike your foot against a stone.'"

Jesus said to him, "Again it is written, 'You shall not put the Lord your God to the test.'"

Again, the devil took him to a very high mountain and showed him all the kingdoms of the world and their glory. And he said to him, "All these I will give you, if you will fall down and worship me."

Then Jesus said to him, "Be gone, Satan! For it is written, 'You shall worship the Lord your God and him only shall you serve.'"

Then the devil left him, and behold, angels came and were ministering to him.

1 Corinthians 10:13 (ESV) – No temptation has overtaken you that is not common to man. God is faithful, and he will not let you be tempted beyond your ability, but with the temptation he will also provide the way of escape, that you may be able to endure it.

Identity Misplacement

Our minds & the enemy want you to believe you are something you are not. You are more than your occupation, a family member, a friend, or any description the earth could give you. You are a child of God and sheep of the Good Shepherd above all else. However, remember to embrace the positions the Lord puts you in that you may bring others to Christ.

Biblical References

1 John 3:2 (ESV) – Beloved, we are God's children now, and what we will be has not yet appeared; but we know that when he appears we shall be like him, because we shall see him as he is.

Psalm 23:1 (ESV) – The Lord is my shepherd; I shall not want.

John 10:14–15 (ESV) – I am the good shepherd. I know my own and my own know me, just as the Father knows me and I know the Father; and I lay down my life for the sheep.

John 17:14–16 (ESV) – I have given them your word, and the world has hated them because they are not of the world, just as I am not of the world. I do not ask that you take them out of the world, but that you keep them from the evil one. They are not of the world, just as I am not of the world.

1 Corinthians 9:22 (ESV) – To the weak I became weak, that I might win the weak. I have become all things to all people, that by all means I might save some.

Part 6: Observation

"Enjoy your new
perspective."

Opening Prayer

Thank You, Lord, for Your continued love, grace, and mercy. Thank You for allowing me to see as You have let me see. Thank You for helping me to continue to choose You.

My heart aches for those who are lost by the tricks of this world. I pray for all those who have no rest in their hearts and minds. I pray for all those who chase money, fame, and pleasure to find and sustain their lives. I pray for those who can't appreciate the blessing You have placed in their lives. Only through You alone, can life fully be enjoyed.

Help me to never lose sight of You no matter my stage or age in life. Help me to be thankful for every person You place in my life. Help me to be grateful for all You provide. Allow me to be more forgiving and love those who can't see more fully. I pray for these things by Your will and Your grace through Christ Jesus. Amen.

I am a sinner, Lord. Forgive me. It is evident that I need You. My full being craves whatever You will allow me to experience as I seek You in silence, though I do not deserve it. Whatever You let me see, hear, or feel, I will be thankful. Seeking Your presence is enough. Your name will continually be on my mind and on my lips.

Choose Wisely

People will be kind if you are kind to them.
They won't share with you if you don't share with them.
People will invite you if you invite them.
They won't trust you if you don't trust them.

You will have friends if you make friends. In the end, the day will come when you get what you give because what you give affects you more than anyone else.

Who Knows?

You could never guess how a person you know may present themselves in the future.

Treat everyone with love, make kindness your norm.

The how, the when, the where, and the why, only the Lord knows.

Meditation VI

Oh lord, there is no end to knowing You.
The more I know, the more I realize Your vastness.
The more I seek You, the more I see that You only reveal
Yourself at the proper times.
Invisible, but visible in a way I could have never
imagined.

How good is Your goodness?
How safe am I in Your shadow?
How rich am I in Your wealth?

All the things I have are only mine for mere moments,
so I praise You for gifting me.
The life I chose was chosen before I even chose it, so I
thank You for choosing me.

Pain will come. Hard times will arise. Tiredness and
fatigue are unavoidable.
Lord, allow me to look to You, come before You, and
desire You always.
For You remain the same, and Your character is flawless.

Lord, guide me, as I am around those who don't know
You as You have blessed me to know You.
In Jesus's Mighty Name, I pray. Amen.

Envy- We become envious of other people because we feel less than, inadequate, or as if we are not enough. Remember you are fearfully and wonderfully made in a unique and intentional way.

Jealousy- We become jealous because we feel as if we should have what someone else has in their possession. We compare our internal self to the external perception of someone else. Find comfort in who made you and all he has given you.

Greed- We become greedy because we do not have the peace of mind that God can and will provide for us.

Anger-We become angry because we want control over a person or situation. When things don't go as we want (since we have no control over what's going on outside of us), we lose control over what's going on inside of us. Release all external control and give it to the creator of all things.

Depression-We become depressed because we lose all hope. The only true freedom is to put your hope in the Lord, not a person, place, or thing. Every finite thing will disappoint you, leave you, or lose its novelty.

Anxiety-We become anxious because we are overly worried about what we don't yet know. We want perfect knowledge and understanding to make decisions and choices that we feel will benefit us. We prioritize the future more than anything else. Instead, trust God that he will work out all of the circumstances and has given you everything you need to move forward with peace while remaining present.

Pride-We become prideful when we are overconfident, have a "God complex," and put ourselves on a pedestal. Through the lens of Christ, may we see our fragility, inherent nothingness, imperfect evil nature, lack of knowledge, and delusion.

Lust-We become convinced that physical sensations or experiences will bring us the joy or novelty we truly desire. Physical pleasure never remains. God is the only thing that sustains.

*There is nothing wrong with feeling these emotions. It's human. Identify them, give them to God, pray, and naturally they will occur less without you actively grading yourself.

The Month Before July

One day, I was walking to get food. When I got close to the restaurant, I stopped and prayed. *Lord, whoever I come across next, I will buy them a meal for you.* I turn around and walk away from the restaurant to stroll around the block. I was close to getting back to the restaurant and didn't see anyone. I turn the last corner and see a person sitting on the steps with green hair, smoking a cigarette. I keep walking past.

At first, I thought to myself. *No way that's the person I am supposed to stop, speak to, and offer kindness.* As I kept walking, the Lord nudged me. In my heart, I heard a message. *You prayed to find a person to bless, and I have provided that person. You dismiss them because of your judgment.* After about ten steps, I turned around and walked up to the person to say hello and told them I wanted to buy them food.

They said, "I'm not poor."

I responded, "It's not about being poor. Sometimes God moves my heart to do good, and you are the person who needs to experience love."

They paused briefly and just stared at me. After a few seconds, they began to talk about their rough day. Their name was June. They lived in a transgender recovery home, and that morning they got into a fight with another person in the house. They felt stressed and needed a break, so they left the house to get some space since the situation felt toxic. As we were getting food, they began to tell me that when they were twenty years old, they were in a car accident with the rest of their family, and they were one of two survivors. They were given half a million dollars, which they spent on houses, cars, and drugs. They told me that they regret blowing through it.

I asked the twenty-eight-year-old, "what would you ask your fifty-year-old self if you could meet briefly?"

June looked at me and immediately said, "I would ask myself if I had found peace."

When we finished ordering our food, I was blessed enough to pay for their meal.

They asked, "what are your motivations in life?"

I told them about my own struggles and personal challenges. Just a few years prior, I had struggled with doing drugs, self-isolating, feeling the need to impress everyone, feeling empty, and trying to escape everything by just being more busy. The only thing that had truly changed the horrible place I was in was my relationship with Christ. I told them about spreading a glimpse of the love I had experienced through finding and maintaining a relationship with Christ. They looked up at me, smiled, and nodded.

They said, "I believe all religions are the same; we just don't realize we are worshipping the same God."

I responded, "I agree that there are truths you can find in every religion. I have studied Hinduism and Buddhism and have many Muslim friends who have taught me about Islam. Nothing compares to the joy, love, peace, and comfort I have found through Jesus Christ."

They stopped and looked at me with this sad introspective look. Finally, they said to me, "you know I have never believed in miracles, but I have had a miraculous day."

I asked them to elaborate. They said, "I live beside a church, and this morning, I saw a Bible on the steps. I didn't think much of it and kept walking. On the bus, there was a Bible behind my seat on the ground. I started to wonder if it was a sign that I should pick it up. And now, you're here, sitting in front of me."

I told June that sometimes miracles are simple. I then urged them, if they were willing, to read Matthew. I thanked them for being so open and vulnerable. We shook hands. I wished them well for the rest of their day, then brought my food home.

I don't know what God will do in that individual's life, but in my own life, it made me realize how much I condemn and judge other people before I ever speak to them or learn their story. If it weren't for God, I would have kept walking and never have given June a chance. Shame on me. I woke up early the following morning and read Revelation 3:20.

"Here I am! I stand at the door and knock. If anyone hears my voice and opens the door, I will come in and eat with that person and they with me."

This invitation is open to anyone and everyone. I pray to God that He blesses that person's life and they receive the peace they desire. Lord, I pray you continue to change my heart and allow me to love all people, even those I would look at and condemn them for being sinners. Who is not a sinner including myself, Lord? Forgive me. Thank you for opening my eyes.

Negative

Jealousy and judgment jade the heart.

To find the deepest states of your mediation. It takes time, commitment, and dedication.

Prevent yourself from saying anything negative about yourself or your situation.

Unforgiving Heart

Our minds & the enemy want you to hold grudges, not forgive, and hold on to other's past offenses. As you get closer to God, you begin to understand how he has freely forgiven you and will continue to forgive you. If you don't forgive others and don't have a willingness to move on, you will feel conviction in your heart for an unwillingness to not extend the grace you were given first to other people.

Biblical References

Ephesians 4:32 (ESV) – Be kind to one another, tenderhearted, forgiving one another, as God in Christ forgave you.

Mark 11:25 (ESV) – And whenever you stand praying, forgive, if you have anything against anyone, so that your Father also who is in heaven may forgive you your trespasses.

Matthew 18:21–22 (ESV) – Then Peter came up and said to him, "Lord, how often will my brother sin against me, and I forgive him? As many as seven times?" Jesus said to him, "I do not say to you seven times, but seventy-seven times."

Matthew 6:15 (ESV) – But if you do not forgive others their trespasses, neither will your Father forgive your trespasses.

Luke 6:37 (ESV) – Judge not, and you will not be judged; condemn not, and you will not be condemned; forgive, and you will be forgiven.

Colossians 3:13 (ESV) – Bearing with one another and, if one has a complaint against another, forgiving each other; as the Lord has forgiven you, so you also must forgive.

Matthew 5:23–24 (ESV) – So if you are offering your gift at the altar and there remember that your brother has something against you, leave your gift there before the altar and go. First be reconciled to your brother and then come and offer your gift.

The more you memorize scripture and hide it in your heart, the easier it is to completely focus on the name of Jesus as you meditate. The beauty of meditation is when you are done. Whatever is on your mind distracting you, you may immediately lift up your voice and earnestly pray to God for help. Handle no thought, emotion, or feeling by yourself. Meditation helps us to be mindful of which areas of our lives need healing, prayer, and transformation.

Biblical References

Romans 12:2 (ESV) – Do not be conformed to this world, but be transformed by the renewal of your mind, that by testing you may discern what is the will of God, what is good and acceptable and perfect.

Unintentional Idolatry

Our minds & the enemy wants us to worship everything with God. In the past, people worshiped idols they created with their hands. Now, people worship fame, money, success, wealth, status, appearance, their jobs, or a person, sometimes without realizing it. It is even possible to idolize or worship the present moment. It is easy to believe that we are smarter than past generations, but we just fall into the same trap in a different way. What you turn to first, rely on, make time for, and allow to shape your life, from your perspective, or think the most about, is what you truly worship. If it is not God, it is an idol. Our minds/the enemy will do their best to convince you that you are keeping God first but be mindful if you are accidentally worshipping or idolizing things or people in this world.

Biblical References

Exodus 20:3 (ESV) – You shall have no other gods before me.

1 John 5:21 (ESV) – Little children, keep yourselves from idols.

Romans 1:21–23 (ESV) – For although they knew God, they did not honor him as God or give thanks to him, but they became futile in their thinking, and their foolish hearts were darkened. Claiming to be wise, they became fools and exchanged the glory of the immortal God for images resembling mortal man and birds and animals and creeping things.

Jonah 2:8 (ESV) – Those who pay regard to vain idols forsake their hope of steadfast love.

Habakkuk 2:18 (ESV) – What profit is an idol when its

maker has shaped it, a metal image, a teacher of lies? For its maker trusts in his own creation when he makes speechless idols!

Galatians 4:8–9 (ESV) – Formerly, when you did not know God, you were enslaved to those that by nature are not gods. But now that you have come to know God, or rather to be known by God, how can you turn back again to the weak and worthless elementary principles of the world, whose slaves you want to be once more?

Isaiah 44:9 (ESV) – All who fashion idols are nothing, and the things they delight in do not profit. Their witnesses neither see nor know that they may be put to shame.

1 Corinthians 10:14 (ESV) – Therefore, my beloved, flee from idolatry.

Part 7: Restoration

"This is where it ends."

Opening Prayer

Blessed are You, Lord our God, King of the Universe.
You breathed into all people the breath of life.
With every breath in I will acknowledge the Father, with
every breath out I will acknowledge the Son, with the
help of the Holy Spirit.
You are the same God.
You command me to come alone to a quiet place and
receive Your rest.
Here I am Lord.
In my solitude I desire Your still small voice. When I'm
still, you move.
In my inactivity, You are active.
In my inability, You are able.
When I am quiet, Your voice is made clear.
When I am silent, You comfort me.
When I am mute, Your majesty is undeniable.
When my eyes are closed, Your eyes are open to all
things.
When my eyes are shut, You guide me through the
darkness.
When my eyes rest, You are there.
You give life to everyone and everything else.
For in you, we live, we move and have our being.
You want us to seek You, reach out to You, and find You,
because You are not far from us.
You are very near.
We are Your offspring, Lord.
So, thank You for placing eternity in my heart.
Thank You for Your Holy Spirit with me now.
Thank You for revealing Yourself through Jesus Christ.
Thank You for this time to meditate.
Thank You for allowing me to sit and be still and know
that You are God.
May Your peace that surpasses all understanding guard

my heart and my mind as I meditate.
Whenever my mind wanders, may You allow me to
refocus my mind on Your Holy Name and on Your
Kingdom that is within me.
May You reveal Your glory as I meditate.
I am a sinner Lord, forgive me of all my sins.
It is evident that I need You.
My full being desires You Lord.
I will be thankful for all things.
Your Name will continually be on my heart, my mind,
my soul, my body, and my spirit.
You are in Your Holy temple.
Allow my silence, the meditation of my heart, and the
stillness of my body to be pleasing to You Lord.

In Jesus Name, Amen.

The Existence Outside of You

There is no time or space.

There is no love or hate.

Only days,

Marvel upon its taste in silence.

May we fully experience the Lord.

Meditation VII

I am broken.
I am weak.
I am moody.
I have wronged my brother.
My faults, my sin, and my issues are before me.
Yet You, Lord, love me all the more anyways.

Thank You for laying down Your life.
Help me to extend more compassion. Allow me to judge
and condemn others less.

Every time I try to look too far forward, I feel anxious.
But every time, I look back, I can give You nothing but
praise. Give me greater security Lord that I am where I
am supposed to be.

No prayer is too small, to stupid, or a waste of Your
time. You hear me, then give comfort and rest to my
soul. Lord, through You, may my gratitude be greater
than my pain, desires, and worries.

Even when I am unsure about everything, there is peace
in your presence.
Take my fear of the unknown away because You are a
God who knows all things.
May my trust in You not depend on what I can see.

You are turning old things new. You have placed my
feet on stable ground. When I needed to hear from
You most Lord, then You spoke to me. This life is too
disappointing to live without You.

Lord Keep my mind from comparing my walk with You
and my journey to others. Help me to accept the things
You allow to happen to me more fully. In You alone, I
find solace. My life is in Your hands. Lord, align my will

with Yours, complete Your work in me, and let Your light radiate in my mind.

May my pace of life be slow, my state of mind be peaceful, and my heart secure in You.
Thank You for the freedom that only exists in You.
Thank You for Your newness every morning. Thank You for holding my hand through every season.

In Jesus Holy Name,
Amen

Ok I Me

One day, I was watching my brother's dog. That morning, I meditated. At some point during the hour, I heard his dog whining because she wanted to go out to pee. I ignored her and eventually she stopped. After I finished meditation, I walked out of the room I had been in, and she was excited to see me and wanted to play. I played with her and my own dog before I took them on a long walk.

From the lens of my brother's dog, she was out of her routine. She was voicing what she felt she needed to do, but when she saw me after she stopped whining, she was filled with joy. Then, more than just being let out to pee, she got to get a lot of steps in.

In the same way, with God, we whine when we want things done on our time and complain when our routines or norms are out of balance, not knowing what he plans for us. When we are in the Lord's presence, we are filled with joy. He has a much greater plan for us than the little we want at this moment. How much less are we as human beings to God? How much more similar are we to the pets we care for?

Attachment

Understand that everything given to you is a gift from God. People, material objects, jobs, careers, and relationships were given and can be taken away. You're simply borrowing these things. They are not truly yours. That being said, you are a human being. You may still get attached. Appreciate your blessings as fully as possible while always giving thanks to God.

Suffering

Some say desire leads to suffering, but doesn't desire lead to true joy at times as well? Savor the joy and give your suffering to God. Those who claim they don't suffer are the ones who suffer from the worst kind of suffering-not being human. This form of suffering is the worst because there are no feelings, no emotions, and nothing truly matters. It is a complete betrayal of your humanity. Reducing yourself to nothing isn't freedom. It is rejection of God who created you, which means you can never be nothing no matter how much you drown things out, distract yourself, or misidentify who you are. Seeking a life free of pain is a life of fear, a life of avoidance, and a life of self-denial that God never intended for us. So, I say suffer because it will never compare to the joy we have from the Lord.

Despite My Knowledge

Despite my knowledge, daily practices, and faith, there are still things I struggle with today. The flesh is powerful no matter who you are or where you are in life. This is why we need Jesus, whether we sin knowingly or unknowingly. I am a sinner, no better than any other person. Thank God for God. Without Him, I would be nothing. The mind will always try to justify why you should do what you are doing. Praise be to God for loving us anyway. Eventually, God's love is so clear that the conviction becomes so overwhelmingly clear. Fighting God is more uncomfortable than anything else. The question remains, submission or pride? In the end, true freedom only exists in God, through Jesus Christ.

Conclusion

After two long, yet seemingly short, years of practicing meditation, I continue to abide in the presence of God. I remain still, silent, and with folded hands and open to listen and receive. Through meditation, so much has changed.

Where I was weak, I became strong. Where I was anxious, I became peaceful. My fear turned into bravery, confidence, and perseverance. It's not that I stopped having problems, but I became more comfortable facing them. My joy was no longer determined by circumstances. My perspective of what truly mattered shifted. Challenging moments felt less overwhelming without losing their meaning, value, or importance. I found solace in knowing that nothing in this world could take away my ability to experience the Lord's presence, and that gave me a hope and strength I never knew I could access.

I realized I have changed vastly. I am more loving, more at peace, more at ease, more prayerful, more thoughtful, more aware of how I act. I desire to serve more, give more, and make sure others are doing well. Finally, I am more open to living presently and I have an increase in purpose in life.

I am no "perfect" Christian. I love Jesus and add Him to the very simple practice of sitting still, not just for myself but to share with others. I want all people, especially those who are willing to give Jesus a chance, to utilize abiding in His presence. Not only is it deeply personally transformative but it opens us up to a relationship with Christ that we cannot experience unless we decide to be silent and be still.

My goal in writing this book is to share my experiences, thoughts, images, and insights that I would not have had without meditation. If all I do is plant a seed in your life, that is enough.

Thank you for joining me on my journey. God bless you.

Closing Prayer

Thank You, God, for this time.
May You allow me to keep this stillness and peace as I leave this place.
Help me to love others as You love.
What are my plans before You Lord?
Keep my mind free from expectation and guide me.
Let Your word marinate in my heart; may Your love surround me.
Allow me to be interested, curious, and fully present in all You allow.
Thank You for the breath in my body.
Thank You for Your Spirit that is with me all day long.
In Jesus name. Amen.

May your meditation leave the seat with you.

May the word of God be seen in how you live.

May you answer others as you desire your prayers to be answered.

Appendix

The Filled Cup

Wants/Desires
Fame-a desire to be known
Status-we desire to be respected
Wealth and riches-we fear á lack in life
Love-we desire to be loved
Titles-we desire to be confirmed by others
Bars, clubs, social events-we desire to belong and be a part of something
Alcohol-we desire to be our full self, fear nothing, and enjoy the moment
Weed-we desire to be calm, relaxed, and ease our minds
Sex Addiction-we desire connection to someone else or validation.
Workaholic-we desire a reason to live
Creativity-we desire to express ourselves
Purpose-we desire self-value
Community/Teams-we desire common goals or shared belief systems
Oversharing-we desire to be heard
Overthinking-we desire control
Identity Crisis-we desire to know who we truly are

Needs/Truths
We are already completely known by God.
God fully respects us because we are His creation.
There is abundant life in God.
God always desires us.
We are enough for the Lord as is.
We are already a part of something great, and the path looks different for everyone.
Through God's love, we may be our full self, have true confidence, and enjoy all things.
True rest is only in the Lord.
We are connected to the creator of all things who we need to prove nothing to.
We were created to fellowship with God and others.
Having a relationship with God allows our existence to be expressed.
Our value is in the fact that we were created, we live, and Christ died for us.
With God, we are already part of an everlasting team.
God is always willing to listen to us through prayer.
By trusting in God, we allow ourselves to enjoy and know that God is in control.
We are God's creation, who loves us enough to die for us.

Some of these desires are unavoidable. Some of these wants are heavily ingrained in our society, culture, or brains. Understanding the root of why we do what we do, want what we want, or desire what we desire gives us the opportunity to slow down and turn to God first to fulfill these needs. This approach to taking care of spiritual desire allows us to enjoy the physical action, want or need, without abusing it. When we realize that everything, we do to feel better is a small bandage for what only God can fix or a small portion of the true experience of God. So, seek out the Lord first, so you can more fully enjoy the things He has blessed us to do here on earth

Human beings are equal parts physical, mental, emotional, and social. We are governed by our spirit, which is intertwined with our being. The spirit is a part of the human body and not a part of the human body at the same time. Don't make it make sense.

Things I Experienced in Deep States of Mediation

Mediation Grunt: a grunt or groan that involuntarily happens. You hear your body make the sound before you realize that it is technically you that made the noise. It is, however, very similar to speaking in tongues but because you're silent when it comes out as a grunt.

1. **Meditative Flinch:** a sudden involuntary body flinch or jump even though you have been perfectly still

2. **Physical Dissonance:** While meditating, you zone out. You are still there. Then, all of a sudden you have a moment when you realize you are in a body. (This is better experienced than felt by words)

3. **Time Unification:** All of sudden, time does not feel like it's passing. It is just as if time just becomes one big moment. The experience of time exists but not in a distinctive separation.

4. **Meditative Vision:** Imagine you are completely awake and dreaming to some capacity. This difference is you see and hear it more than you are watching it. You are in the dream.

5. **Light Beyond the Dark:** I meditate in very dark rooms with candlelight and salt lamps as the primary source of light. However, in the darkness of my closed eyes and dimly lit room, there is a golden, bright, warm light that pierces through the darkness. It's as if I can see the light beyond the darkness. The darkness is not dark enough for this light.

www.ingramcontent.com/pod-product-compliance
Lightning Source LLC
Chambersburg PA
CBHW051321120626
46547CB00015B/2332